Moon Kids

by Mary F. Blehl
illustrated by Jeff Hopkins

MW01108979

PEARSON

Scott
Foresman

Editorial Offices: Glenview, Illinois • Parsippany, New Jersey • New York, New York
Sales Offices: Needham, Massachusetts • Duluth, Georgia • Glenview, Illinois
Coppell, Texas • Ontario, California • Mesa, Arizona

Every effort has been made to secure permission and provide appropriate credit for photographic material. The publisher deeply regrets any omission and pledges to correct errors called to its attention in subsequent editions.

Unless otherwise acknowledged, all photographs are the property of Scott Foresman, a division of Pearson Education.

Illustrations by Jeff Hopkins

Photograph 24 NASA

ISBN: 0-328-13617-4

4 5 6 7 8 9 10 V0G1 14 13 12 11 10 09 08 07 06

It was mid-year when the "Moon kids" arrived. That's what the students in Ms. Blake's Earth science class called the kids who had come from the moon.

Lakeland School had been chosen by the government as a site for an exchange program with people living on the moon. A colony was set up there as an experiment by several countries. The goal of the colony was to see if people actually could live there in buildings underneath the lunar surface. Some people there didn't speak English, and the kids on the moon spoke the language of the country of their parents. They all tried to learn English in order to communicate with each other, and some were better than others.

In class that day everyone was sitting on desks or chatting with their friends in the dingy classroom, waiting for their teacher, Ms. Blake. The whole school was buzzing about the kids who had just come from the moon for a month.

Allen Thomas and Mark Lopez sat closest to one of the Moon kids.

"What's your name?" Allen asked the tall Moon boy, who was sitting staring into space. The Moon boy looked a little pale. Allen thought he might be tired after his long journey.

The boy answered "Peter."

"What do you do for fun on the moon?" was Allen's next question. The boy didn't speak much English, so Allen tried to act out what he meant. Peter shook his head to show he didn't understand.

The bell rang and Ms. Blake came into the room.

"Take your seats, everyone," she directed. As soon as the class was seated, she announced, "We have some new students with us today. They are from the moon. Let's make them feel welcome. Where is Peter?"

Peter just sat there. The other students stared. "Peter?" she asked again, more loudly and clearly this time. Peter tilted his head to the right.

"Graham?" she asked. The second boy did the same.

"Celia?" she asked of the girl and got the same response.

When all the other students had given their names to the new students, Ms. Blake continued.

"Today we will discuss our class project. You will all form groups and decide on a science-related project. At the end of the month, we will hold a science fair."

* * * * *

Later, at lunch, Allen and Mark were sitting in the cafeteria talking about their science project.

"I can't believe Ms. Blake put us in a group with the Moon kids," said Allen. "How are we ever going to get this project done when they can't even speak English?"

"I don't know," replied Mark, always the optimistic one. "I'm sure we'll figure something out."

"Well, I guess we can start by asking them to come over after school tomorrow," said Allen.

"Fine by me," said Mark.

After school Allen and Mark found Peter and Graham in the hall by the lockers.

"Can you guys come over to my house after school tomorrow to start on the project?" asked Allen.

Peter looked at him blankly.

"I'll draw a picture," Allen said, taking out his notebook. He drew a picture of a house and a tree and a stick figure. "Allen," he said, pointing to the stick figure.

"Allen," repeated Graham.

"House," Allen added, pointing to the house.

"House," repeated Peter.

Then Mark grabbed the pen and drew a clock. He put the short hand on the three and the long hand on twelve.

"Three o'clock," said Mark. The Moon boys stared at him. Then Mark held up three fingers.

Peter and Graham stared at the fingers and said nothing; Mark and Allen had no idea if they understood.

"Why don't we go see how Jennifer is doing with Celia?" asked Allen.

Mark and Allen went to find their friend Jennifer with Graham and Peter close behind. They found her playing a word game with Celia. Celia was pointing to something, and Jennifer was telling her what it was. Celia pointed to Jennifer's hair.

"Hair," said Jennifer, touching her hair and then Celia's.

"She must have a lot of hats at home," commented Mark.

"Why is that?" Allen asked.

"Because the moon gets down to −360 degrees at night," replied Mark. "Maybe they don't even go outside after the Earth goes down. Ha! Get it? The sun goes down here, but the Earth goes down there."

"I get it," responded Allen. "Hey, Celia, can you and Jennifer come over to my house tomorrow after school?" He held out the picture of the house he had drawn. Then Mark showed her the picture of the clock that said three.

Celia understood and nodded her head.

"Great!" said Allen.

The Earth kids waved goodbye and turned to leave. The Moon kids only nodded and followed them to the school entrance.

As they walked out of the school toward the buses, the Moon kids started tripping over their feet.

"What's with them?" asked Allen.

"They don't walk much on the moon," said Jennifer. "They do a lot of jumping because on the moon they weigh about one-sixth of what they weigh here. You can jump higher, so you can travel more quickly."

Outside a man was waiting for the Moon kids.

"I am Sergeant Campbell. Are you friends of theirs?" he said, nodding toward the Moon kids.

"We're trying to work on a science project together. Do you think that they can come over to my house tomorrow so we can get started?"

"I will make sure their parents know about your request and will meet you here tomorrow after school."

"I live about a mile from here," said Mark. "We can all walk together if that's all right with you."

"I will take you, so I know where to pick them up," said the sergeant.

The next day they all gathered at Allen's house. Jennifer brought science books she had checked out of the library. The Moon kids looked over the contents of theirs without a word.

"You guys are very quiet," Jennifer said to Celia. "Don't you like the book you have?"

"I don't think it's that," said Allen before Celia could answer. "Since there is no air on the moon you can't hear anything there. I read somewhere that you have to have a special type of walkie-talkie to hear someone talk to you. Or you have to be in a room where there is air."

"Hey, I just got an idea!" exclaimed Mark. "Why don't we do a project on the lunar eclipse that's coming up?"

"Yeah!" said Allen. "My sister works at the Northern University observatory. Maybe we could get in and use the telescope! We could watch the moon wax and wane!"

"No!" said Peter and Graham together.

"Why not?" asked Jennifer.

"Dark bad. Stay inside," said Celia.

"What's she talking about?" asked Allen.

"A moon night lasts for two weeks," said Mark. "I would imagine that it's very easy to get lost in the dark on the moon."

"Well, what else can we do? It doesn't look like we can negotiate with the Moon kids on this one," said Jennifer. As she was speaking the sky began to turn dark.

The Earth kids left the table and ran over to the window. Celia, Peter, and Graham looked terrified as thunder rolled across the sky.

"It's only thunder," Allen reassured them. Then lightning lit up the darkness. "Come and see." The Moon kids hesitated but finally went to the window.

Then the rain started to fall. The smell of it began to waft through the open window. They filled their hands with rain and splashed it on their faces. Celia stuck out her tongue to catch the rain on it.

"Good!" she said.

"Hey, listen to this!" cried Mark, holding up his book. "It says here that there is no weather on the moon!"

"How can you have no weather?" asked Allen.

"It says that because Earth has gravity, it holds the clouds above the planet. The clouds hold water to make rain or snow. The sunlight comes through the atmosphere and it looks like blue sky to us. On the moon the sky isn't blue because there is no atmosphere."

"So if there is no atmosphere on the moon, then the sky must be black," said Jennifer.

By the time the rain stopped everybody's clothes were wet. The children decided to go home and change. They would meet about the project another day.

"Well, did we decide to do a project on weather?" asked Allen.

"Why don't we keep track of things like temperature and rainfall for a few days?" said Mark. "We can compare the weather here with the weather in, say, Japan."

"We could each take a time of day for our records. Allen can record the weather in the morning, Mark in the afternoon, and I'll take the evening," suggested Jennifer.

"What are these guys going to do?" Allen said.

"Maybe they could help with the posters at the end. Can you draw?" asked Allen, turning to Celia.

"Draw," answered Celia, nodding and making circles in the air.

"Sounds good to me," said Jennifer. "I'll start keeping track of the night sky tonight."

* * * * *

The weather project was a success, and the Moon-Earth team won first prize at the judging. The Moon kids had even gotten over their fear of the night and had come to the award ceremony.

The science fair signaled the end of the month. The Moon kids would soon go home.

The next day the principal informed everyone about the other half of the exchange program. Because the Moon-Earth team had been so good at working together, Jennifer, Allen, and Mark were asked to go to the moon. Each of them would bring one parent.

Ms. Blake was going too. A few weeks later, she called a meeting for everyone making the trip.

"We need to review some of the differences between our two environments. Everyone will have to be outfitted with a special spacesuit."

Ms. Blake had a suit laid out on the table in front of her and invited everyone in front to get a closer look.

"These things weigh a ton," said Jennifer as she lifted the helmet.

The suit covered every part of the body. The temperature on the moon varies from extremely cold to extremely hot: the suit would insulate them from the cold and cool them in the heat.

"Will we have to sleep in these suits?" asked Mr. Thomas, Allen's father.

"Once you get inside the lunar house, or module, there will be air circulating," answered Ms. Blake.

"You'll have to get a second set of clothes to take with you to wear on the moon," continued Ms. Blake. "Make sure they are one size bigger than what you wear now."

"Why do we need bigger clothes?" asked Mrs. Lopez, Mark's mother.

"There is no gravity to pull our bones together. Everybody is going to stretch!" Ms. Blake replied.

Ms. Blake went on to show pictures of the lunar housing. "Everything is built underground," she explained.

"Why did they build the lunar structures underground?" said Mrs. Lopez.

"Because of the extreme temperatures. It can go from −360 degrees Fahrenheit at night to 260 degrees during the day," explained Ms. Blake. "Does anyone else have a question? No? Then tomorrow we'll begin preparations for our flight next month!"

The following month they took off from Cape Canaveral in Florida. Once they were in space, the captain let the passengers take off their seat belts. Everyone floated up to the top of the room inside the shuttle and bumped the ceiling.

"I've never felt so light," said Mrs. Kay. She gave Jennifer a push, who rolled and spun like a paper airplane.

When it was dinner time, the travelers held their food instead of putting it on a plate. "I always wanted to eat with my hands," said Allen.

A couple of Earth days later, the captain announced, "Please put on your spacesuits in preparation for our arrival!"

Looking out the shuttle window, everything was black. The surface of the moon came into view and they could make out a large dent in the soft rock. It was a crater, which had the entrance to the housing module in its center.

"It looks pretty spooky out there," said Jennifer.

"What day is it on the moon?" asked Allen's father.

"One day on the Moon lasts fourteen of our days," said the captain. "So you'll really be here only two moon days, instead of twenty-eight Earth days."

About ten minutes before landing, the captain came on the intercom. "We will be leaving the shuttle in about thirty minutes. From there we will go into the underground structure, where we will be staying."

The view of outer space was amazing, especially of the planet Earth; it was a beautiful blue with white swirls curling around it.

They descended into the lunar housing module where they would live for the next four Earth weeks. The first place they reached was the spacesuit closet. They took off their spacesuits and went into the next room.

Peter, Graham, and Celia were there to welcome the Earth expedition. There were a lot of hugs, high fives, and exuberant greetings exchanged.

"Come see our home," said Celia to the little group. Her English had improved since her stay on Earth. "Use the handles on the wall to get around."

"This is our living area," Celia explained while the parents talked to each other. "Here are our TV and Internet. Snacks are in the wall."

"Do you play sports?" asked Allen.

"Yes, we exercise every day," answered Graham.

"Why is that?" asked Mark.

"Muscles are weak here," explained Peter. "Less gravity."

"OK, so what else do you do here?" Allen asked.

"Eat three meals, walk outside," responded Graham. "Read books, do homework, clean partition." There wasn't enough space for people to have their own rooms, so instead there were partitions to separate the beds.

"Any parties?" asked Mark.

"Once a year we have special birthday cake," said Celia. "Parties not often. We save food for every day."

"I guess you have a problem getting food here. What happens if the space shuttle doesn't get here?" asked Allen.

"We have a greenhouse specially constructed for the moon," said Mr. Landers, the head of the colony, who had overheard Allen's question. "The plants grow very quickly when it is daylight here. We heat the greenhouse during the moon nights."

The moon families then took their guests to the eating area, where they served them freeze-dried ice cream. It tasted strange to the visitors from Earth.

After the snack Mr. Landers announced, "Today you are free to roam the module, but make sure you read the signs on the doors first," he cautioned. "You only want the rooms that have air in them."

Peter and Graham wanted to show the boys the whole module. The first level was for daily meals and recreation. The second level, which looked like a gymnasium, was where they exercised. The bottom level was the training area for expeditions outside the module.

The next morning the Earth children untied themselves from their beds. They had tied themselves down the night before in case they moved too quickly in their sleep and floated away. Because there was less gravity, there was less force pulling them down with their every motion.

Everyone met for breakfast in the living area. There was milk inside the wall, and cereal came in little packages that they attached to the wall to get a squirt of milk.

After breakfast the group went into the lower level for their first exercise class.

"Why do we have to go to exercise class so soon?" asked Jennifer.

"A lot of your strength comes from gravity," said Mr. Thomas. "The muscles are naturally strong from the gravitational force on Earth. Here there is a weaker force, so the muscles become weak."

Throughout the class everyone was amazed at how their muscles didn't get tired as they worked. There was less gravity pulling down on them.

After class there was quiet time for reading, and then everyone met for lunch. The afternoon was spent at a lecture about the stars that could be seen from the moon but not Earth. A periscope that reached the surface from inside the room let the children see the stars that the instructor was talking about.

The next Earth day everyone was going to learn how to use the lunar flying device that would allow them to traverse long distances on the surface of the moon.

The three Earth kids and their parents went to the training room. It was completely bare except for padding on the walls and ceiling. There was no air in this room, so everyone had on spacesuits.

"Today you will learn how to propel yourself using these devices with special combustion engines," announced Mr. Landers. "The device is attached to the inside of your sleeve. It's just like a video game. The controls have arrows in four directions. When you press the up arrow, you will go up." He demonstrated going up and back down. "Give it a try."

Allen pressed his up arrow too hard and bumped his head. Mark went sideways and collided with his father.

After about a half-hour of practice, Mr. Landers announced, "OK, I think you guys have it. Does anybody have any questions?"

"Where are we going today?" asked Jennifer.

"Our trip today will be exactly one mile from the module. We will visit the highlands, a place where there are mountains almost as tall as Mount Everest. Our goal is to take some photographs with a special ultra-violet camera. Since there is no reflected light during the moon's night, NASA had to invent a special camera. We will take turns taking photos."

"Can we walk instead of fly?" asked Mark.

"Yes, you can," replied Mr. Landers. "Just make sure you keep up with the rest of us."

Mr. Landers opened the doors, and everyone flew out into the open. Allen felt like a feather, tumbling through space. Without the clouds and sky above his head, there was no limit to how far he could see.

Mr. Landers was keeping his body fairly near the ground. They were going in a huge circle in front of the the subterranean door from which they had exited. They flew around for about an hour and then returned to the training room.

"Good job, everyone," said Mr. Landers. "I think you're ready to try a trip to the highlands. Just stay behind me. If you have any trouble, come up next to me, and I'll try to help you."

It was an even eerier feeling for the Earth kids when they exited the module this time. No one went down to walk on the moon dirt. They were all too scared to be left behind, so they stayed in line behind Mr. Landers.

When they arrived at the base of the highlands, if they had had any breath, it would have been taken away. The mountains were silhouetted against the starry black of the universe. They kept their lunar devices in "static" mode and touched the soil with their feet for the first time. It was slippery, but all of the visitors got to make an imprint with their feet for everyone in the future to see. Because there is no dust or wind on the moon to erase them, they knew their footprints would stay on the moon forever.

The Moon

Humans have always been fascinated by the moon. When Galileo improved the telescope in 1609, it was suddenly possible to see the moon much more clearly. Galileo saw what looked like mountains and seas. He also saw craters, or places that looked like holes, in the moon's surface.

We have always known that the moon looks different at different times of the month. The moon waxes and wanes because Earth casts a shadow on the moon. The shadow changes the appearance of the moon in different ways as Earth revolves around the sun and the moon revolves around Earth.

Although the moon is very large, it is not a planet. It is a satellite of Earth, because it orbits our planet. If Earth were a basketball, the moon would be the size of a baseball. It takes about a month for the moon to revolve around Earth.

In 1969 Neil Armstrong became the first person to set foot on the moon. People watched this historic event on television all around the world. It was then that he spoke the famous line, "That's one small step for man, one giant leap for mankind."

Illustrations by Jeff Hopkins

Photograph 24 NASA

ISBN: 0-328-13617-4

4 5 6 7 8 9 10 V0G1 14 13 12 11 10 09 08 07 06

Every effort has been made to secure permission and provide appropriate credit for photographic material. The publisher deeply regrets any omission and pledges to correct errors called to its attention in subsequent editions.

Unless otherwise acknowledged, all photographs are the property of Scott Foresman, a division of Pearson Education.

Illustrations by Jeff Hopkins

Photograph 24 NASA

ISBN: 0-328-13617-4

4 5 6 7 8 9 10 V0G1 14 13 12 11 10 09 08 07 06